Amphibiana

# Slimy SALAMANDERS

by Meish Goldish

Consultant: Dr. Kenneth L. Krysko
Senior Biological Scientist, Division of Herpetology
Florida Museum of Natural History, University of Florida

New York, New York

**Credits**

Cover and Title Page, © Lynda Richardson/CORBIS, cloki/Shutterstock, and Sergey Chushkin/Shutterstock; TOC, © James DeBoer/Shutterstock; 4, © Parke John/Visuals Unlimited, Inc.; 5, © Michiel Schaap/Minden Pictures; 6T, © Breck P. Kent/Animals Animals Enterprises; 6B, © age fotostock/SuperStock; 7T, © Tom C. Amon/Shutterstock; 7B, © age fotostock/SuperStock; 8, © Sebastian Kennerknecht/Minden Pictures; 9, © Biosphoto/Véchot Christophe/Peter Arnold Inc.; 10, © Song Jianchun/Imagine China; 11T, © Fanny Reno/Shutterstock; 11B, © David M. Dennis/Animals Animals Enterprises; 12, © Susan Yates/Alamy; 13, © Fritz Rauschenbach/mauritius images; 14, © Sebastian Kennerknecht/Minden Pictures; 15, © Byron Jorjorian/Alamy; 16, © Dwight Kuhn Photography; 17, © Matt Meadows/Peter Arnold Inc.; 18, © Dwight Kuhn Photography; 19, © Dr. Paul Zahl/Photo Researchers, Inc.; 20T, © Dwight Kuhn Photography; 20B, © E. R. Degginger/Photo Researchers, Inc.; 21T, © Gary Meszaros/Photo Researchers, Inc.; 21B, © David M. Dennis/Animals Animals Enterprises; 22T, © Jane Burton/Bruce Coleman Inc./Alamy; 22B, © Ken Lucas/Ardea.com; Back Cover, © James DeBoer/Shutterstock.

Publisher: Kenn Goin
Editorial Director: Adam Siegel
Creative Director: Spencer Brinker
Design: Debrah Kaiser
Photo Researcher: Picture Perfect Professionals, LLC

*Library of Congress Cataloging-in-Publication Data*

Goldish, Meish.
Slimy salamanders / by Meish Goldish.
p. cm. — (Amphibiana)
Includes bibliographical references and index.
ISBN-13: 978-1-936087-37-2 (library binding)
ISBN-10: 1-936087-37-5 (library binding)
1. Salamanders—Juvenile literature. 2. Salamanders—Life cycles—Juvenile literature. I. Title.
QL668.C2G56 2010
597.8′5—dc22
2009035941

For more information, write to Bearport Publishing Company, Inc., 101 Fifth Avenue, Suite 6R, New York, New York 10003. Printed in the United States of America in North Mankato, Minnesota.

112009
090309CGB

10 9 8 7 6 5 4 3 2 1

# Contents

# Living in Flames?

Thousands of years ago, people in Europe burned logs to cook food and stay warm. As the fire burned, they often saw **slimy** little creatures scurry out of the flames. The people thought these animals were created by the fire and gave them the name *salamander*. The name comes from a Greek word which means "living in flames."

Salamanders are among the earliest known animals on Earth. They first lived at the same time as dinosaurs, about 165 million years ago.

▲ Old, rotting logs are popular homes for many kinds of salamanders.

Of course, people now know that salamanders don't really live in fire. Many of the creatures simply like to live or hide inside logs. If the logs are burned, the salamanders rush out to escape.

**The fire salamander is one of the most common kinds of salamanders found in Europe today. Its name is a reminder of the time when people thought salamanders lived in fire.**

# Water Animals

Salamanders are actually just about the opposite of fire animals. Because they are a type of **amphibian**, they are really water animals.

The word *amphibian* means "a double life." Amphibians were given that name because during their lives, most of them live in two different **habitats**—one in water and one on land. They usually spend their early life in water and their adult life on land.

**The mudpuppy is one kind of salamander that spends its entire life in water.**

**The spotted salamander is one of the most well-known salamanders that spends its adult life on land.**

Water is important to salamanders and all other amphibians. It keeps their skin **moist**. The animals aren't just covered and protected by their wet skin. They also use it to breathe in **oxygen**. If their skin dries out, they will not be able to get enough oxygen—and they will die.

Like salamanders, frogs and toads are also amphibians.

# Cool, Wet Homes

There are about 380 different **species** of salamanders. All of them need to keep their bodies from drying out, but they are able to do so while living in different kinds of habitats.

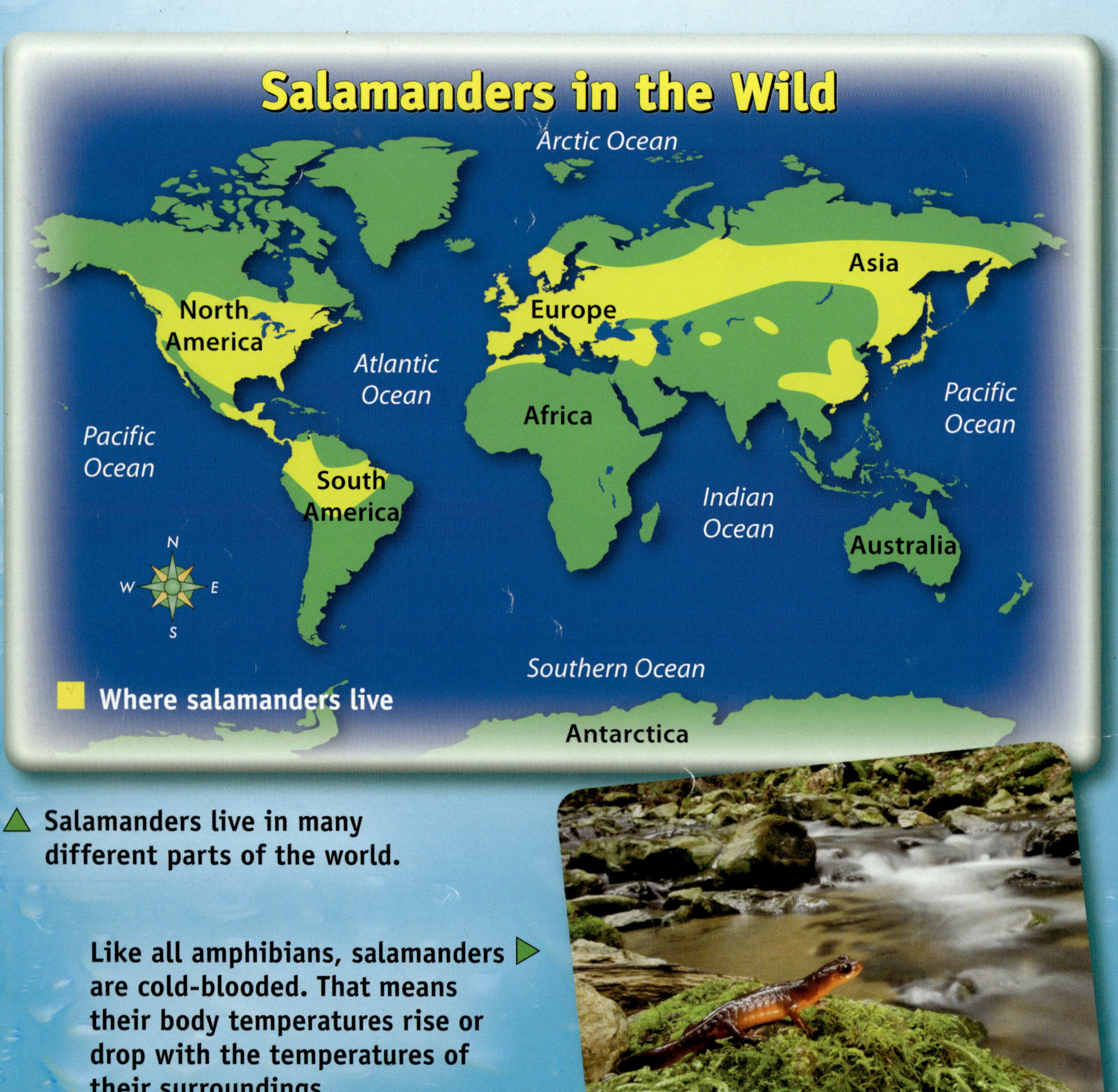


▲ Salamanders live in many different parts of the world.

Like all amphibians, salamanders are cold-blooded. That means their body temperatures rise or drop with the temperatures of their surroundings. ▶

Some salamanders live their entire lives in water, in places such as ponds and streams. Others live all or most of their lives on land, but always in wet, well-shaded areas—for example, under rocks, leaves, and logs. They usually hide during the day to keep out of the hot sun. At night or on rainy days, when the air is cooler, they come out to look for food.

During the winter, many salamanders **hibernate** to escape the freezing cold. Those in water bury themselves in mud to keep warm. Those on land dig into the ground or settle under logs or rocks.

**One kind of salamander—the olm—lives inside caves. Olms stay in total darkness in underground pools within their tunnel-like homes.**

# A Closer Look

A salamander, like its home, is always cool and damp. The skin on its long body and tail is slimy because it is covered by a thin layer of mucus. The mucus helps keep the skin from drying out.

▲ The biggest salamander is the Chinese giant salamander. It can grow to at least five feet (1.5 m) long.

Because of their shape, salamanders are often mistaken for lizards. The two creatures aren't related, however, and are different in many ways. A lizard is a kind of **reptile** that has claws and rough, dry skin with **scales**. A salamander has no claws or scales. Its smooth, wet skin is much more like a frog's than a lizard's.

Like all lizards, the green iguana is covered with scales.

Most adult salamanders are between three and six inches (7.6 and 15.2 cm) long. They usually have four short legs. Some kinds that live in water, however, may have only two.

One of the smallest salamanders is the pygmy salamander, which can be as tiny as one inch (2.5 cm) long.

# Favorite Foods

Salamanders hunt other animals for food. Smaller salamanders go after insects, spiders, worms, snails, and small fish. Larger salamanders also eat snakes, mice, and frogs. Some salamanders, such as spring salamanders, even eat other salamanders!

A salamander has teeth to hold on to prey, but doesn't use them to chew its food into small pieces. After biting its prey, it simply swallows it whole.

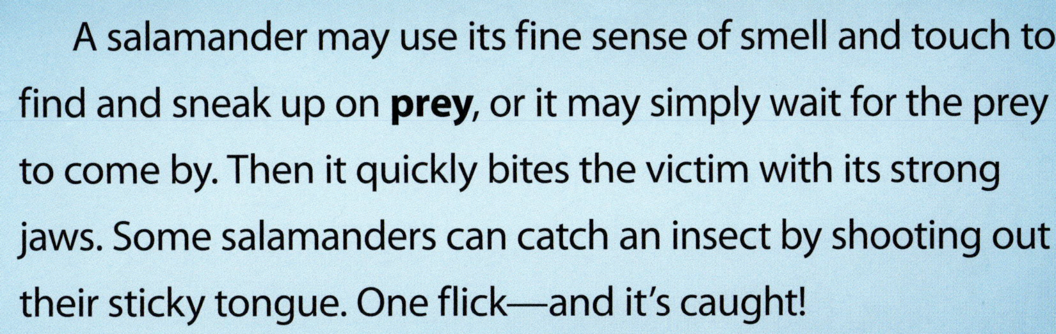

A salamander may use its fine sense of smell and touch to find and sneak up on **prey**, or it may simply wait for the prey to come by. Then it quickly bites the victim with its strong jaws. Some salamanders can catch an insect by shooting out their sticky tongue. One flick—and it's caught!

**The fire salamander catches insects with its quick tongue.**

Salamanders drink through their skin. They soak up water while in a pond or sitting on the wet ground.

# Keeping Safe

Many hungry **predators**, including snakes, birds, and frogs, will eat salamanders. However, salamanders have several different ways to keep safe. They usually come out only at night, when it's hard to see them. Some species blend in with their surroundings because of their colors and markings. These patterns make them even harder to spot!

**The colors of this long-toed salamander make it hard for enemies to see it on land.**

The slime on salamanders also protects them. It tastes bad and often is **poisonous**. Many of these poisonous salamanders also have bright colors that act as warnings to hungry animals. After a predator has tried to eat one of these creatures, it remembers the animal's bright colors and bad taste. If it sees the salamander again, the colors remind it to stay away.

The bright color of this salamander tells other animals it is poisonous.

If grabbed by a predator, a salamander can lose its tail or leg and escape. The salamander grows a new tail or leg in two to ten weeks to replace the one it lost.

# Sticky Eggs

Most salamanders—even those living on land—go to a pond or stream to **mate**. After mating, the female usually lays her eggs in or near the water. The eggs are covered with a clear, sticky jelly that holds them together. Often, the eggs also stick to twigs, rocks, or logs in the water.

Salamander eggs are held together by a sticky jelly.

Many species of salamanders lay hundreds of eggs at a time. A large number of eggs helps the creatures survive, since many of the eggs are eaten by birds, snakes, fish, turtles, and raccoons. The eggs that stay safe usually hatch after four to six weeks.

Salamanders that do not lay their eggs in water lay them under rocks or in other damp spots on land.

▲ **Most salamanders that lay eggs on land don't stay with them. However, a few kinds, such as this four-toed salamander, guard their eggs until they hatch.**

# Baby Salamanders

Baby salamanders that come from eggs in the water hatch as **larvae**. They have no legs at first, but they do have **gills** for breathing, just like fish. The gills take in oxygen from the water.

**Salamander larvae use gills to breathe in the water.**

Salamanders that come from eggs on land develop in a different way. They hatch with legs and without gills. They breathe through millions of tiny holes in their skin. Some kinds of baby salamanders that live on land also have **lungs** to take in air.

Red-backed baby salamanders hatching on land

All baby salamanders, whether they hatch in water or on land, have tails. Babies that hatch in water use their tails to swim.

# Growing and Changing

After a few weeks, salamander larvae that hatched in water go through big changes. Scientists call what happens **metamorphosis**, which means a "change in form."

Salamanders don't all change in the same way, however. Most larvae lose their gills and develop lungs, which they will use along with their skin to breathe. A few species, however, keep their gills as adults. The larvae also grow legs—usually four but in some cases only two.

## Life Cycle of a Spotted Salamander

1 The mother lays her eggs in a pond in the spring.

2 The eggs hatch in about 5 weeks.

The different ways salamanders grow and take shape prepare them to survive. After all, some of these amphibians will never leave the water, while others will spend their whole lives on land. Most kinds, however, will live up to their name and lead a double life—leaving the water and moving onto land.

3 The baby salamander stays in the water for about 12 weeks. It uses its gills to breathe underwater and begins to grow legs.

Salamanders can live up to 35 years. Some that are kept in zoos or as pets have lived up to 55 years.

4 By late summer, the salamander has lost its gills, grown legs, and moved onto land as an adult.

# Salamanders in Danger

Salamanders have been on Earth for millions of years. However, scientists fear that some species may now be in danger of becoming **extinct** due to diseases or changes in the **environment**.

Because salamanders take in air and water through their skin, they are especially sensitive to **pollution**. Also, as more ponds and streams are drained to make way for new buildings, more salamanders lose their homes and places to mate.

In some parts of the world, certain kinds of salamanders are already extinct. Here are two kinds that are currently in danger.

## Axolotl (ak-suh-LAH-tuhl)

- This salamander is found in central Mexico.
- The axolotl stays in water all its life. It is now threatened by pollution.
- In 1998, there were about 1,500 axolotls per square mile (2.6 sq km) in the waters where it lived. Today there are only 25 axolotls per square mile (2.6 sq km).

## Chinese Giant Salamander

- This salamander lives in the mountain streams and lakes of China.
- The Chinese giant salamander is threatened by people who hunt it for food.
- The building of dams in China has led to a loss of homes for these giant salamanders.
- In the past 50 years, the number of Chinese giant salamanders has shrunk by 80 percent.

# Glossary

**amphibian** (am-FIB-ee-uhn) an animal that usually spends part of its life in water and part on land

**environment** (en-VYE-ruhn-muhnt) the area where an animal or plant lives, and all the things, such as weather, that affect that place

**extinct** (ek-STINGKT) when a kind of plant or animal has died out

**gills** (GILZ) the body parts of a water animal that are used for breathing

**habitats** (HAB-uh-tats) places in nature where animals are found

**hibernate** (HYE-bur-nayt) to spend the winter in a deep sleep to escape the cold

**larvae** (LAR-vee) baby salamanders after they hatch from eggs

**lungs** (LUHNGZ) the body parts of an animal used for breathing

**mate** (MAYT) to come together to produce young

**metamorphosis** (*met*-uh-MOR-fuh-siss) the change that salamanders and other amphibians go through from egg to adult

**moist** (MOIST) slightly wet

**oxygen** (OK-suh-juhn) a colorless gas found in the air and water

**poisonous** (POI-zuhn-uss) able to kill or harm an animal or person if eaten

**pollution** (puh-LOO-shuhn) harmful materials that damage the air, water, and soil

**predators** (PRED-uh-turz) animals that hunt and kill other animals for food

**prey** (PRAY) an animal that is hunted by another animal for food

**reptile** (REP-tile) a cold-blooded animal, such as a lizard, snake, turtle, or crocodile, that uses lungs to breathe and usually has dry, scaly skin

**scales** (SKAYLZ) small pieces of hard skin that cover the body of some animals, including fish and reptiles

**slimy** (SLYE-mee) soft and slippery

**species** (SPEE-sheez) groups that animals are divided into, according to similar characteristics; members of the same species can have offspring together

# Index



# Bibliography

**Clarke, Dr. Barry.** *Amphibian*. New York: DK Publishing (2005).

**Edmonds, Devin.** *Newts and Salamanders*. Neptune City, NJ: T.F.H. Publications (2009).

**Hofrichter, Robert.** *Amphibians: The World of Frogs, Toads, Salamanders, and Newts*. Buffalo, NY: Firefly Books (2000).

# Read More

**Bredeson, Carmen.** *Fun Facts About Salamanders!* Berkeley Heights, NJ: Enslow (2008).

**Maruska, Edward J.** *Salamanders*. Chanhassen, MN: Child's World (2007).

**Nelson, Robin.** *Salamanders*. Minneapolis, MN: Lerner (2009).

# Learn More Online

To learn more about salamanders, visit
**www.bearportpublishing.com/Amphibiana**

# About the Author

Meish Goldish has written more than 200 books for children. He lives in Brooklyn, New York.